THE FIGHT FOR MY LIFE

What I Discovered as I
Triumphed Through Tragedy

TRICIA WYNN PAYNE

Dedication

To all of the people who have helped me triumph through tragedy:

My parents who first taught me that God is real, my siblings who strive always to protect me, my nieces and nephews who stand as my motivation for writing,

my loving extended family who undergird me,

my clergy sisters, close friends, and vast church family who prayed for me.

————————————

To my loving husband Shawn, thank you for loving me back to life.

.

Acknowledgements

The writing of this book would not have been possible without the help of several individuals: Lexi Johnson, thank you for asking the question that finally propelled me forward from the bleachers to the pen, and for making the perfect introduction. Joan T Randall, you believed in me and coached me from concept to reality. Roxana Bell, your scrupulous eye will never be forgotten. Yvonne McIntyre Collins, thank you for insisting that I journal. I extend my deepest gratitude to my parents, Courtney and Joan Wynn, for planting the first seed in my heart to write. My mother-in-law Dee, for raising a remarkable son. Lastly, my dear husband Shawn, I appreciate you for doing more to care for us, so that I could take the time to write our story.

TABLE OF CONTENTS

INTRODUCTION

People have looked at me and declared, "You don't look like what you've been through!" They have wondered, "How did you get through that?" Many encouraging me have said, "You should write your story and share it!"

Now, let's be clear, I would be dishonest if I did not admit that I have had moments of anger, questioning, and deep hurt over what happened. Sometimes I still feel upset, but then I remember the good. Yes, even in the midst of tragedy, I found goodness. Veritably, as I trusted in God's help, I learned some of the greatest good is discovered after experiencing adversity. Out of our pain, and the many tragedies we face living on this planet, God works it out so that in the end, our pain serves a greater purpose.

It is with this faith, that I write and share my story. I believe that there is at least one person who needs to hear how God brought me through and continues to bring me through each day. So, I write this for those who have ever faced or are currently in a sudden "storm," difficulty or, adverse circumstance. May you not only survive the storm, but triumph through it. May the great God in Heaven who knew you even while you were in your mother's womb, speak to you and hold you through your difficulty. May the words of this book bring you encouragement, equip you to exit this storm with peace, a greater purpose and with a deeper faith in God.

PART I

The Fight

CHAPTER ONE

THE UNEXPECTED

BEEP! BEEP! BEEP! BEEP!

My heart raced, pounding as if it would jump right out of my body. Pain gripped me mercilessly, holding me prisoner, powerless. What in the world is happening to me? I thought as the room swarmed with white coats and green scrubs. What was all of the fuss about? Feeling confused, I watched them scurry like determined ants. Wait a minute, this is about me!

I sensed the panic in the room, swelling by the second. The expression on their faces, all directed at me, confirmed my worst nightmare–it's a fatal emergency. Fright overwhelmed me, and I looked at Shawn. Appearing just as alarmed, Shawn gazed at me, seemingly helpless to change the unfolding scene. Something was terribly wrong. Sweeping in the room with haste, the doctor explained, "We have to reset her heart. Where's the husband?" Like a student in class, Shawn raised his hand, "Right here!" With his attention directed at Shawn, the doctor urged, "Ok it's your job to keep her here."

Holding my hand with intense tenderness and strength, Shawn fixed his eyes on mine and started talking. I can't remember what he said, but our conversation rose above the dread-filled air in the room. In that moment, it was just me and my husband of only one and a half years. Still newlyweds, still in love. My room buzzed with what seemed like the entire staff from the floor. This was my ground zero.

I had seen reactions like this before, about 15 years earlier. Filled with new graduate excitement and youthful vigor, I embarked upon my first full-time professional physical therapy career working on the acute care and in the intensive care units. It wouldn't be long before what I read about in my textbooks, would be observed and in some cases, acted out by me as a physical therapist. An alarm would sound from the patient monitor and in dashes the nurse. Then another alarm pings and an announcement blares overhead. Like college sprinters, an entire team runs together to a patient's room, with one mission in mind—save life.

Now I was the patient. Turning his attention toward me, the physician explained, "Tricia, this will probably hurt; it won't feel good." The doctor was about to reset my heart's rhythm, and they had to act quickly. Unbeknownst to me, my heart threatened to race me right out of existence.

Shawn continued his conversation with me, seeming to ignore the crowd of worried medical professionals. Like lovers in the park, we kept talking, but for a moment he stood alone, and I was gone. Shawn describes it as the single most frightening moment of his life. The moment that his wife's life seemed to slip out of his hands. For me, I felt nothing. I heard nothing, I sensed nothing, and I said nothing. There was absolutely nothing, as my heart slowed to a near halt and was then slowly brought back.

I understand well the concept that death is like a thief that surprises us, stealing. In one instant you are here–breathing, hearing, talking, smelling, and feeling–and in the next moment gone. Ecclesiastes 9:12 says, "People can never predict when hard times might come. Like fish in a net or birds in a trap, people are caught by sudden tragedy." I was caught! How in the world did I get here from months of abdominal pain diagnosed as ovarian torsion, to undergoing a diagnostic pelvic laparoscopy due to persistent discomfort, to now having my heart reset by panic-stricken nurses and doctors?

Just a year prior, I married a wonderful man, was officially commissioned as a pastor in the Gospel ministry and nearly to the date, I preached at our denomination's annual

Pastoral Leadership and Evangelism Counsel. The Holy Spirit moved in such a mighty and powerful way that 120 pastors and leaders gathered afterward to continue in prayer. I would have never imagined that after such a year of blessing, near the end of the following year, I would find myself fighting for my life, and it all started with the onset of sudden abdominal pain months earlier.

CHAPTER TWO

IT'S NOT JUST PAIN

Terror gripped me as I nearly fainted on the cold bathroom floor. I was home alone and frightened by what came as suddenly as a tsunami. Reaching for my phone, I called Shawn, "Babe, I think I am going to have to go to the hospital." Hanging up, I dialed 9-1-1. "Hello, what's your emergency?" The voice on the other end sounded calm and distant. I explained the best I could, wondering all the while if I was overreacting, yet certain I needed immediate medical attention. I felt so scared, frightened by the severity of the pain. *I've never experienced pain like this before*, I thought. "Please, I'm in pain. I need help."

Having nearly passed out, I knew something was terribly wrong. I had never experienced such symptoms. I've incurred sport injuries from my past athletic days and never had pain like this, nor nearly fainted because of it. As a physical therapy student, I was definitely not a fainter, not at the sight of blood, when watching heart surgeries performed, knees replaced or when working on cadavers.

The paramedics arrived, assessed, and took me to the hospital. The pain continued. As I watched the hospital workers frantically dash from room to room, to the nursing station, and again from room to room in the ER, I knew that only God would be able to help me. With training in the sciences, I knew that the experts had one level of understanding in pathology, but if God is not in the mix, people can go down the wrong diagnostic path. Lying there in the hallway on a bed, I prayed, holding my hand over my throbbing abdomen. After numerous tests and assessments, they sent me home with a probable diagnosis, ovarian torsion, and a prognosis of recovery within a week.

I continued to follow up with my OBGYN who assured me that this malaise would resolve within a few days, but it did not. Instead, the pain grew worse. Multiple visits to my doctor coupled with numerous diagnostic imaging tests, provided no reasonable answer. I kept pushing through it, working through it, traveling and attending meetings, still hurting. The final step, as determined by my OBGYN was to take a look inside by way of a diagnostic pelvic laparoscopy, reasonably moving from least invasive to more invasive procedures. After months of pain, I agreed. Such pain should not be ignored. It is the body's way of letting us know that something needs attention. If the pain goes unaddressed the outcome could be disastrous.

The procedure scheduled, we arrived on time to sign the necessary paperwork. The morning of November 29, 2017 seemed like any other day. They completed the simple probe, without any reasonable findings to account for the level of agony I had been experiencing over the previous months. With instructions and prescriptions in hand, Shawn took me home to recover over the next few days. Unbeknownst to us, that would be the last "normal" day we enjoyed that year. We walked in the outpatient diagnostic facility not having a clue that this would be the beginning of the greatest test of our faith, our marriage, and our life.

Chapter Three

NOW THIS?

O nce we arrived home, the pain did not
go away, it only grew more excruciating. No position Shawn tried to rest me in
proved beneficial nor gave relief. I writhed
in agony. Determined to help, Shawn called
the doctor multiple times about my post-op
complaint. With new instructions to modify
the timing of my pain medications and the
addition of another, Shawn tried to nurse me
back to health. Soon the urge to use the bathroom, prompted me to try to get out of bed.
As I stood with Shawn's help, I felt my

strength leave, as I collapsed to the floor. Darkness.

Opening my eyes, I saw a confused and worried husband hovering over me, lifting me off of the ground. I can't remember if I ever made it to the bathroom. Something was wrong. We just did not know how wrong, and we would never have imagined that this discomfort was indicative of a life-threatening emergency. Immersed in unusual pain and increasing distress, the night inched along slowly.

Early the next morning, Ana, a very concerned friend, came over to check on me. Looking at me, and hearing about the night of pain I had, she opened up and shared a very personal story about her father's unfortunate and untimely death as a result of a simple thing that if caught early, would have saved his life. She encouraged us to go to the ER. Without hesitation, grabbing coats and bags, Shawn packed us up, and the three of us headed to the ER only a few minutes away.

Silently, I wondered if all of this was necessary. Maybe the doctor was right and this was normal after a diagnostic laparoscopy. Had Ana not come by and shared her story, I would have stayed home, underestimating the severity of my condition, and would have likely died there. Burying his head in the computer, the emergency room physician reviewed my chart. This ER visit felt different from the first one months earlier in a chaotic emergency room, I was diagnosed with ovarian torsion. This time, I sensed peace in my room. Turning his attention to me, the doctor asked a few questions about my recent pelvic laparoscopy. After he listened to my answers, his disposition leaned toward sending me home. I prayed, *Lord, please help this doctor make the right call.*

Even though we live in the 21st century, and the United States has had a Black president, I was very aware that research demonstrates that Black people receive less attentive care in hospitals as compared to others, particularly when it comes to complaints of pain. Afraid that I would become another unfortunate statistic, I continued to pray, *Lord, please let this doctor make the right call.* At this point, I knew I needed a more comprehensive work-up.

Looking at the ER doctor, I continued to pray, *God, I don't trust in human wisdom or strength, but I trust in You. We need Your intervention, Your help. Help me God!* Immediately, I sensed God's peace. Directing his attention to Ana and Shawn, the doctor asked, "What do you do?" Ana replied, "I'm an attorney." Shawn followed, "I work with medical software." After a moment of silence, the ER physician spoke, "Okay, we will transport you over to the women's hospital for observation."

After a short ambulance ride, I was admitted to the Women's Hospital. Looking at me, with what seemed like a great measure of disbelief, the nursing staff pushed me to walk, attributing my suffering to gas and immobility. Getting up, I tried to walk, but the pain gripped me relentlessly. *Do they think I'm being lazy?* I wondered. I grew more frustrated, perceiving that my complaint was being dismissed. I silently questioned if my race played into the staff's reluctance to provide greater assistance. Feeling no better, my status declined further. Days passed. Then it happened, my room suddenly swarmed with green scrubs and white coats.

The medical team finally found that my body had suffered an internal injury so damaging, that my organs were shutting down. In what was supposed to be a simple outpatient laparoscopy, a portion of my small bowel became perforated during the procedure. For three days, the contents of my bowels had spilled out, spreading throughout my abdominal cavity leading to peritonitis. Infected, my blood had become a conduit of death instead of life. The pain I had experienced the day I left the outpatient facility was not normal, and I was not overreacting. No matter what schedule I followed in taking the pain medication, it would have never fixed my problem.

Chapter Four

INTERVENTION

What I was experiencing was not gas or as a result of immobility. Had I stayed home, I would have died there. Had the doctor sent me home and not admitted me, I would have died days later. Had my friend not shared her story about her father's unfortunate passing as a result of not having a simple examination by a medical professional, I would have died at home thinking that I was overreacting and that the pain was normal after having an outpatient laparoscopy. Had my husband Shawn, not been there for me, I would have died.

Months before, even before my first trip to the ER, I sensed a life storm was coming. While in prayer, I sensed God directing me to pray for myself. As a pastor, I had grown very accustomed to praying for the ministry and my congregation while neglecting myself. But leading up to this great tragedy, I was directed to pray for myself. I expected a storm, and I even knew it would pertain to my health, but I would, nor could have ever imagined that it would be this devastating. Nor could I have ever anticipated the complications that would arise as a result.

When it became apparent that something was terribly wrong, I knew I needed special spiritual and family support. First, our parents needed to be notified. However, how do you inform your elderly parents that their previously healthy, strong, and independent baby daughter went from having a minor procedure to being admitted in the hospital on the brink of death? Shawn had the challenging task of making the call and communicating in such a way as to alert them to the urgency while protecting them from the severity of the situation since both have health challenges of their own, in addition to the over 500-mile drive to be present. Next, we needed extra special spiritual support.

"Shawn," I said, "please call Aunt Yvonne." Yvonne had taken special interest in me seven years prior upon first meeting me. I knew then that there was something rare about this woman. She had a larger than life heart, and her connection to God was so strong you could almost see the ribbon that connected them. I knew I needed her by our side. We needed her presence and prayers. Without hesitation, she hopped on a plane and stayed with us for days. Laying her hands over my abdomen, she prayed. This was not the first time I received such prayer.

A month earlier, while the diagnosed ovarian torsion pain was still unresolved, I attended a week-long ministry meeting out of town. I knew that I would see the prayer ministry coordinator of our division, Pastor James, and one of my spiritual mentors whom I respect deeply, Pastor Brenda. I was determined to ask them to pray for me. I saw

James first, and asked him if he would have special prayer for me and anoint me.

"I've got to call my wife," James said, as he quickly reached for his phone. "We have been praying for you over the past five weeks!" He went on to explain that the Lord had impressed him to pray for me five weeks prior to that moment. As I counted back five weeks, I realized that Pastor James began praying for me around the day I nearly fainted in excruciating abdominal pain, right before I first called 911. I stood speechless because I had no prior communication with Pastor James. Only God could have revealed that to him. A couple days later, both James and Brenda prayed and anointed me with oil, and they continued praying for me daily.

Two weeks after that encounter, I unex-pectedly bumped into another Spirit-filled individual, pastor and friend, Andrea, while attending a different ministry conference. I admired Andrea, not only as a trailblazing fe-male pastor, but for her deep faith in God, so when I saw her, my heart filled with excite-ment at the chance to reconnect. I told her about my ongoing challenge with unresolved abdominal discomfort. "Anoint yourself," she said, directing me to anoint myself with oil over the very place that, unbeknownst to me, would become my place of injury. Then she prayed. One can never have too much prayer. Two and a half weeks later, Shawn and I traveled to be with family for Thanksgiving, where I would receive prayer and be anointed a final time.

The abdominal pain continued as we traveled to be with our family for the Thanksgiving holiday, but by this time the laparoscopy had been scheduled as no diagnostic test revealed the cause. After the Sabbath Thanksgiving service, we spent time with Joe and Nordia, the pastor and first lady of Shawn's home church. Being very spiritual people, they resolved to pray for me. Nordia, took the anointing oil and rubbed it on my abdomen as they prayed. Again, the oil was placed on the very place that would days later be the place of life-threatening injury. In retrospect, as I write, I can see God's hand was with me all along. At that time, I did not realize the magnitude of the battle that awaited me ahead, but God knew. God was making a way of escape for me.

However, when the surgeon explained that I must undergo emergency small bowel repair, I did not recall the previous prayer encounters. Emergency surgery was unimaginable to me. How did I go from a simple outpatient diagnostic laparoscopy procedure, to becoming septic and now losing a part of my small bowel? My body would never be the same again!

The surgery was performed, but I remained in critical condition. I would go on to spend about a week in the cardiac intensive care unit. I have little memory of these immediate post-operative days and of the time spent in the cardiac ICU, but I remember, I felt like dying.

"Lord," I said, "I have given all of my best years to You. I have been preaching Your Gospel for over 20 years. I have fought a good fight. I'm tired now." I could feel life leaving me, and I was okay with that.

I left everything I loved on this earth to pursue God's call to serve in pastoral ministry. I left my native country, parents, siblings, nieces, and nephews. I even left my profession as a physical therapist. None of that compared to my love for God and my desire to obey Him. But now, I felt tired and beat. *Surely there are many others that could preach and lead,* I thought. *Perhaps this was my time to go,* I concluded. *Perhaps, it was time to rest, and close my eyes, only to open it again to see the face of Jesus upon His return.* I prayed that I would meet Him in peace, but then I looked up.

There standing by my bedside was my husband of not yet two years. Looking at him, I realized that there was still more to live for; much more life ahead, yet to be experienced. We just started our life together and I did not want it to end prematurely. *Lord, I want to live!* I said silently in prayer. God heard. Like a sudden detour from a road leading to a dead end, my status turned for the better. I was soon moved from the cardiac ICU to a regular acute care medical floor. However, I had many more milestones to cross before I would be deemed stable to return home.

"Do you want the television on?" the nurse asked, as she noticed my days were spent mostly lying in bed in total silence, an unusual sight for a young woman. "No, thank you," I replied. The nurses likely thought I was crazy to lie there in the room in silence, but to prevent this tragedy from destroying my hope and my sanity, I remained in constant prayer and did not want CNN or Fox to distract me. The humor of *Black-ish* or the drama of *Secretary of State* would not help. During these moments in the hospital, the entertainment could serve as a rude mind invader if I let it, interrupting my prayer communication with God. What even my husband did not know, was that when I was not sleeping, I remained in constant communion with God. Not yet strong enough to read my Bible or devotional or journal, I communed incessantly with God. And He was revealing, even the very contents of this book.

Chapter Five

COMPLICATIONS

"Tricia, you've got to try to walk more," the nurse said. "I'm trying," I responded, "but I'm having a difficult time breathing, and it hurts." Motioning to my left side, I directed her attention to a new area of pain. The incentive spirometer sat on my bedside tray, challenging me to inhale deeply and slowly. The doctor was clear; I should try to aim for 2000 ml and try to keep the indicator steady as I inhale.

I was familiar with the incentive spirometer. For years, I coached my acute care patients on its use, and now it was my turn. *This would be easy*, I thought. I was in for a rude awakening. I understood that deep breathing would be important to keep my lungs clear and open, and to prevent further complications. With that understanding, I tried. What looked easy turned out to be extremely difficult. I could barely move the indicator near 500 ml, less than a fourth of where I should be. My lungs were barely expanding. Most certainly the lower portion of my lungs received little to no air. I was either still too weak to breathe deeply, or something else inhibited me. My full-hearted attempts appeared so meager. I couldn't inhale easily. Challenged to try every hour, I was met with constant defeat.

When the doctor came in to check on my progress, I felt like a student during an exam, nervously aiming to prove I measured up. But I did not. "Keep trying," my surgeon advised. Again, I felt like I failed, and hoped I was not being perceived as a noncompliant and lazy patient. I just couldn't move it. The medical staff's instructions resounded,

"Keep trying!" "Get moving!" "Walk." I was being challenged.

"I can't breathe," I said. "Something is wrong," I told my nurse. *Are they listening to me?* I wondered. The nurse continued to encourage me, "Okay, keep trying to walk." I tried.

As I walked with the staff, I continued more firmly, "It hurts." Again, motioning to my left side. On another attempt to walk the hall, a sharp young physician swept up to me. "Show me where it hurts," she said. I again motioned to my side.

"Okay," she said. As if a light went off, she assessed me. She swept away just as quickly as she came. Before I knew it, new orders were in. Shortly after, I was sent off for further diagnostic testing. The finding? Pleural effusion, and it was not pretty.

The porter transported me from my hospital room, to a procedure area in a completely different wing and floor of the hospital. There, the technician relieved me of the thick pale green fluid that filled my pleural cavities (the space between my lungs and chest wall) compressing my lungs and making it impossible for me to inhale fully. I could not bear to look after about 60 ml of thick green fluid filled a syringe. Seeing that only impressed upon me further the severity of my sickness. The porter returned me to my room, however breathing easier and grateful. Soon the incentive spirometer would reveal that I was not lazy and non-compliant. However, that horrific gross green intruder was not limited to my lung area.

My days in the hospital were somewhat surreal, or perhaps more like a night terror. As if having heart and lung issues were not enough, it became apparent to me that my abdominal incision developed more than an infection. The wound nurse did not have to say it; I knew. As they worked to change my dressing, yellow drainage along with incisional separation could be seen. Further, brown-green drainage accompanied by a putrid odor very obviously, oozed from my lower abdomen. This lower part of my incision, where the rank brown-green substance poured out, concerned me the most. *What in the world is that?* I thought. The wound nurse was reluctant to say.

On his regular rounds, the surgeon inspected my incision. "What's happening?" I asked, knowing something was awfully wrong. The doctor explained, "Well... you've developed a fistula." "A fistula?" I asked, "What's that?" The surgeon would go on to explain that bowel contents were being rerouted and emptying through my incision instead of staying in my intestines and emptying where it should, in the toilet. For days upon days, intestinal contents were soaking my healing abdominal incision. "How long will this take to heal?" I asked. The answer depressed me. "Well, with fistulas, we don't know. That could take a while." I knew from his tone, that I might have to live with this.

I was not prepared for these sudden changes of circumstances. Everything was happening so fast. I went from independent, medication free, and healthy, to bedridden, heavily dosed by a variety of life-supporting medications, with lines and tubes hanging from every direction. For not only were my lungs and abdominal incision invaded by the gross green stuff, but also my abdominal cavity. A catheter bag, the size of the foley catheter used to collect my urine, was now attached to collect the fecal matter pouring from my abdominal incision. Yet we would soon discover, even further complications.

I continued to have pain, mostly along my left side. By now, my complaints of pain were taken seriously and quickly acted upon. The medical staff came to realize that I remained in tune with my body and my subjective complaints were reliable. When I indicated that I was in discomfort or pain, tests were scheduled. Taken so frequently to tests and procedures, I became very familiar with the transporter (or porter) staff.

One porter in particular seemed to pick me up for most of my procedures, and not by chance. We quickly developed a great rapport. She was a Christian woman and soon our conversations would reveal that I was a pastor. However, as she transported me, she became my pastor. "Could you read to me?" I asked. She spoke of her daily devotional, and it interested me. At this point, visitors were limited, and I needed encouragement.

Pulling up her daily reading from her smartphone, she read, we prayed, and I was encouraged. God knew I needed this, for after each test, it seemed I was met with more bad news.

"Everything that could go wrong, did go wrong," my surgeon explained sitting by my bedside. As he made his daily rounds, he told me of new complications. "As we were operating on you, your bowel contents were leaking, and you formed abscesses in your abdominal cavity." In my body's attempt to contain the outpour of rancid fecal matter, pockets of infected fluid formed resulting in a new area of pain. Soon, more tubes with bulbs on the end were attached to drain, yet more gross green stuff. I felt like I was in a scene from a sci-fi thriller with all of these attachments.

There I was, lying in bed donned in that awful blue-green hospital gown, paired with yellow socks, an unattractive brown bonnet on my head, IV's lines, tubes, and bags hanging in all directions. Instead of Shawn lying snuggled up next to me, he huddled in the chair by my window refusing to spend one night at home without his wife. What an odd turn of events for newlyweds. Who could have imagined that not even two years after exchanging our vows, they would be tested to this extreme? I did not look close to the woman he married.

Chapter Six

SUSTAINED BY LOVE

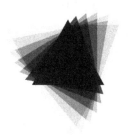

On our wedding day, my silken black hair, swept along my perfectly powdered brow, curved my blushed cheeks and danced gently about my shoulders as I took each step toward Shawn. Tears of joy threatened to interrupt the flawless flow of spring tones as my eyes mingled with anxious anticipation and earnest emotion. My father and I stepped in rehearsed rhythm to Canon in D, as he led me to the crest of this new chapter. Shawn's eyes lit with such earnest as his 5'7" 135-pound bride approached in an ivory laced, floor length trumpet style, sweet-heart trimmed wedding dress. The veil flowed over my shoulders, draping my small hour-glass shaped body and trailed on the ground three feet behind. Silk, crinoline and lace covered my thin modestly toned legs as my French tipped toes peeked out with each step in silver jeweled heels.

Now, I could barely recognize myself. My legs resembled that of an elephant's trunk, and my body was suddenly larger than it had ever been before. Within days I gained over 60 pounds of water weight. As I looked down at myself, the only thing reminding me I was still a lady was the red nail polish on my toes a reminder of my mother-in-law Dee's Thanksgiving pedicure gift. While I previously practiced modesty in appearance, down to my toes, this time, unbeknownst to me, my daring break from neutral tones, to bright red, would serve as a source of hope. Even though I did not feel like it, nor look like it, that red toenail polish reminded me that I was still a woman and still a wife. Even when I found myself in tears and soaked in my own urine.

"Nurse! I need to go to the bathroom." I had gained enough strength to be able to stand and take a few steps with assistance. The foley catheter collecting my urine, was discontinued and I was being encouraged to use the toilet, or bedside commode. Excited to be moving in the right direction, I did not resist. However, this posed a new problem. I had to wait for assistance. The yellow socks on my feet served as a rude reminder that I was a fall risk and not permitted to get up to mobilize on my own. Shawn was not permitted to assist me because of all the lines and tubes attached, so I had to wait. I wanted to be able to wait.

"Shawn," I called out embarrassed as he stood over me, "I don't think I can hold it." Within a few minutes, a nursing staff member appeared, but it was too late. I was soaked. My gown was soaked. My sheets were soaked. My bed was soaked. In tears, I cried, "I'm so sorry. I tried to hold it." Utterly humiliated and embarrassed, I cried. Feeling less than a lady, I cried. So sad to give the nursing staff yet more work, I cried. Confused and in disbelief at what was happening to me, I cried. As I was being cleaned up, I looked at my toes-red nail polish. I smiled to myself. *I am still a lady.* Somehow, Shawn still treated me like a lady and cherished me as his wife.

Several times during our hospital stay, without being asked, Shawn took a wash-cloth, a basin filled with warm water, and some hospital soap, and began washing my feet. It would be weeks before we returned home, weeks without a shower or a bath, but Shawn helped me retain some dignity and feel loved as he washed my feet. With such love and tenderness, Shawn lived his vows to me spoken not even two years before. Yet, I did not know just how discouraged my condition led me to feel, until the day our family arrived.

When my parents came, I did not know whether to smile or cry. I think I did both. Now sitting by my bedside after driving over 500 miles, my mother looked at me and gently said, "Tricia, I didn't know you were this sick!" My beautiful mother retired after over 35 years of nursing work; she recognized a sick person when she saw one. Her youngest child was sick. Dad stood over me silent. I cannot begin to imagine how this made them feel.

Almost 40 years earlier, my parents made the difficult decision to allow their baby girl to undergo surgery where the odds of survival to success were split down the middle at 50/50. They stood by my bedside then as I recovered from that major life-threatening surgery which I am unable to recall. If not for the scars, I would never know that I was operated on as an infant. At only 6 months, I underwent abdominal exploratory surgery leaving a scar which stretched the length of my abdomen. That life-saving surgery led to the discovery of a benign tumor the size of an orange, which if left untreated would have resulted in cardiac failure and death. Now, almost 40 years later, mom and dad looked on in utter disbelief as their previously healthy adult baby girl lay sick in another hospital bed.

My spirits soared at the sight of my parents, and the tender presence of my mother proved better than medicine. As though functioning as a member of the nursing staff,

41

my mother Joan, reverted back to her nursing days, and began caring for me. Her loving hand placed the blankets perfectly about her daughter's morphed frame. Tenderly, she cleaned my face and with her care warmed my heart. There's nothing like a mother's love.

My big sister, niece, and brother also took the trip. My eldest brother, unable to travel, called without fail daily. Their presence served like therapy. With hearts filled with faith and prayer, they surrounded me with love. My brother, Curtis, tuned up gospel hits which healed my soul. Olivia, my niece, assisted me in performing exercises left by my physical therapist. My big sister Deon ensured my physical and emotional comfort. Gary, my eldest brother called daily, giving Shawn much needed emotional support, and Dad prayed deeply in his heart for a miracle. My mother-in-law, arriving in a moment's notice, tended to my care with as much concern as she would give her own child.

All of this loving support from those closest to me served as a catalyst for my healing not just spiritually and emotionally, but also physically. In sickness, Shawn still cherished me. I was sustained by love. However, this was just the beginning of my road to recovery. Soon our family would return to their home miles away. While night after night Shawn tried finding rest in a hard chair, as the nurses and doctors cared for me, there would be days and weeks ahead when just Shawn would be responsible for my care. We could never have foretold what these days ahead would be like for us, but they were coming, whether we were ready or not.

CHAPTER SEVEN

ANTICIPATION

The Christmas holidays were quickly approaching, and the social worker came to speak of discharge plans. *I know this drill*, I said to myself. I could not imagine going home in the condition I was in. I understood that with the holidays came vacation time for staff. People rarely want to work over the holidays, and I imagined the hospital would be thinly staffed. What did all of this mean? They needed to discharge as many stable or near stable people as they could, and after over three weeks in the hospital, my name was considered.

Shawn seemed optimistic and confident that he could handle a sick wife at home. I was less enthusiastic about it as I looked down at my still healing abdominal incision, draining fistula with bag in place. Two JP drains (Jackson-Pratt used for collecting bodily fluids) still emptying the abdominal abscess, the PICC line (Peripherally Inserted Central Catheter, used for long-term intravenous care) coming out of my chest, and the line through which I was receiving my daily yellow shake. Not yet permitted to eat, my nutrition was pushed through a tube and I was still feeling very weak and very afraid. *I didn't come in like this, how in the world can I leave like this? Too many variables*, I thought. *Too many things that could go wrong, with no one to monitor us at home*, I feared. I was not independent and still needed supervision and assistance. The social worker assured us that home care nursing would be established, and they would come to help us. What we were unprepared for was the coming storm that awaited us once we made it home.

With everything attached I was guided to sit in a wheelchair, and wheeled out to the front door, still in shock that I was actually going home like this. It was December in the Midwest, and in the middle of a winter blast fitted with both cold temperatures and steady snow. *How in the world were we going to manage?* I wondered to myself, *Shawn is not a nurse, and all of our family lives hundreds of miles away.* I did not feel ready to leave. Looking at the winter blast outside, I nervously waited for Shawn to help me to the car. It was freezing. *Now*, I thought, *brace yourself for the ride home.*

My entire abdomen still sore, I felt every bump and pebble on that road. The ten-minute drive from the hospital to our home doubled yet seemed more like an hour as Shawn drove carefully while the snow continued to fall, merciless to our plight. When we finally pulled up, I felt happy and relieved to see our house for the first time in weeks. *Now*, I thought, *how would I walk the 200 feet from the car to our front door when I had yet to walk 50 feet?* This distance looked daunting, but like newlyweds all over again, Shawn took me. With his arm locked in mine, he held me tightly as I leaned on him, and we slowly took one step after another through the Midwest winter blast. Soon 200 feet lessened to 150 feet and then to 100 feet, and eventually we made it to the door. As Shawn opened the door, the sight of home warmed my heart, feeling like sunshine on a summer's day. We were home, our home. I sighed with relief, but soon we would have to face the rude reality of my medical needs unaided by 24-hour nursing support.

When I looked inside, it was obvious that Shawn gave careful thought to my return home, rearranging the furniture to accommodate me. I sat in a chair in our living room that Shawn thoughtfully set up. I sat there for hours as we awaited the home care nurse promised to arrive that day. When she finally arrived, emerging from winter's blast, at about 9:00 p.m., we were both tired. She gave us a crash course in triple lumen PICC line care, tube feed management, intravenous antibiotic administration, wound and dressing care, and JP drain care. The instructions given were to be followed exactly, especially as it pertained to the IV antibiotic and tube feed administration. If it was not followed exactly, the results could be fatal.

Presumedly, I should have been able to follow these instructions myself for my own care, however, there is no way I was in any physical or mental condition to administer my own care at this point. My husband Shawn would be my night and day nurse. He would now be my doctor, rounding every four to eight hours to ensure my proper care, unbeknownst to me sacrificing his day job to make caring for me his full-time job. It was a one-man show, with no one else present to tag in, or with whom to change a shift. What I did not realize at the time, was just how many people were praying for us, calling, and providing support to Shawn from a distance.

Shawn executed his new duties like an experienced nurse, prepping, priming, injecting, administering, and repeating on time around the clock. He even set me up with a walkie talkie radio to alert him if a need should arise. He had it down. My life depended upon his care, and he did not let me down. Like a nursing baby gazes into the eyes of her mother, I fixed my gaze upon this man God gave me for such a time as this as he stood patiently over me, slowly and carefully, administering my life supporting medications. *If a man can love like this*, I thought, *how much more God?* Even in my worst condition, I felt the love of God through my husband. *Somehow*, I thought, *this will all be worth it in the end*. However, soon my medical needs surpassed even Shawn's very capable care.

"Shawn, I'm in more pain." Words I dreaded saying. Words Shawn dreaded hearing. Something else was wrong. "What do you want me to do?" Shawn asked lovingly. It was now Christmas Eve, the night of his birthday. We were home for almost three days, and we both wanted this nightmare to end. However, I learned not to ignore pain from everything that previously transpired. Yet, even this still required quite a bit of inner strength and determination to push past my inclination to minimize my pain and instead express my need for help. "I think I need to go back to the hospital Shawn." Looking defeated, he sighed, "Okay." Once again, he packed us up and we headed back to the emergency room.

My husband did his very best to manage my care at home doing an amazing job handling the complexity of my care, but we did not know that among other things, my drainage tubes, purposed to clear the infected fluid from the abdominal abscesses, had become occluded. I needed further medical attention.

After the standard four-hour ER work-up and assessment, without hesitation this time, I was admitted on the very early hours of Christmas morning. My favorite holiday and Shawn's birthday felt less than festive and overshadowed by this health crisis. However, brighter days awaited us ahead, if we could just press through this without giving up. Victory was just around the corner if we would persist and not surrender to defeat.

Chapter Eight

PROGRESS

"Hello, I am the chaplain, and they have asked me to come and speak with you about advanced directives and end of life planning." Sitting at my bedside rather stoic, the chaplain spoke with almost no feeling in her voice. "Advanced directives?" I questioned fully confused by this visit by the chaplain who did not even offer to pray with me, or ask me how I was doing, or encourage me in my very obvious health crisis. "Am I dying?" I asked.

During my previous stay, before being sent home days earlier, I had not been visited by a chaplain. As a pastor, I welcomed the consolation, comfort, and prayers of sincere clergy, but I was met by surprise this time. The hospital chaplain divorced from compassion came to speak with me about advanced directives. "No," she said, "You are not dying." Relieved, I admitted, "I am in no mental condition at present to discuss advanced directives, but I would love it if you would give me a Bible and offer prayer for me."

Surprised that I did not have a Bible, she left the room quickly and returned just as rapidly with a Bible in hand, coupled with a look of astonished disappointment. She had learned I was a pastor. "How is it that you don't have a Bible?" she asked. What she did not know, was up until this point, I was unable to focus long enough to read. I was too sick and sleepy. Her prayer offered no comfort, but that Bible she gave me did. Like a child on Christmas morning, I opened it as though discovering the Bible for the first time. The words on the pages began to speak to me in ways they had never before, and I would begin to learn new lessons and redis-cover old ones that took on new meaning.

Over the next week, I progressed stead-ily, physically, getting in and out of bed with increasing independence, and walking the hall further and further on my own with IV pole, tubes, and bags attached. I progressed steadily mentally. Shawn now trusted me with my phone to read and respond to mes-sages. I progressed spiritually, fortifying my mind with Bible promises that would even-tually serve to take my faith in God to new depths while in the midst of this tragedy. As the week neared an end, I felt ready to go home.

Seeing my improvement, the surgeon thought I should transition off of the tube feed and clear fluids to attempt eating a reg-ular meal. *Real food!* I thought to myself, *I can't wait to try!* After a forced fast from reg-ular food for about 28 days, I was ready. "Or-der a tray." The instruction of my physician need not be repeated. "Start slowly, maybe with soup," the nurse cautioned. My early at-tempts at eating, met with some difficulty, required a few tries before the food stayed down. My nurse's furrowed brow, as she mumbled "bowel obstruction" under her breath, let me know that I would be met with challenges and a long journey to recovery ahead. "You will have a one percent chance yearly of a bowel obstruction for the rest of your life," the surgeon later warned. *Well*, I thought to myself, *that's a 99% chance that I will be okay.* While I did not know it then, happier days awaited me, but only after a period of struggle.

Arm locked in arm, leaning on Shawn, again we walked from the car to the front door. This time, while cold, the weather seemed more favorable. I entered our home with one less apparatus to worry about, *I can eat!* I thought joyfully. *No more feed tube!* I felt like an Olympic marathon runner completing a competition in first place as we entered our home. Now, however, a new kind of struggle began.

The surgeon did his part, the hospital supporting medical staff did their part, the home care nurse, aide, and therapist would do their part, but this leg of recovery rested largely upon me. Up until now, I just determined to have the will to live, but now I needed to act upon the reality that God indeed spared my life and healed me while I was being healed. This required a type of faith I had yet to ever experience. A type of faith that began to grow as a result of my time spent reading that Bible, the emotionally detached hospital chaplain provided.

My wounds were still in the process of healing, oozing, and in need of care. Shawn still had to administer IV meds through my PICC line like an experienced nurse and ensure I took my meds on time daily. I still tolerated very little activity and could do little for myself. The fistula still drained, my skin still scaled by weeks of dry dead skin, but I had to act upon my belief that I was healed while still healing. The day the physical therapist came to my home brought me face to face with this very reality.

Leading the exercises that at one time I myself would have given my own patients, the physical therapist instructed me to try to perform these several times daily. I thought he was crazy. *Lift my buttocks how many*

times? Didn't he know what happened to me?
I could barely lift my buttocks once. Surprised by my failure to launch, I wondered how I could ever repeat these 10 times. I could not believe just how weakened my core became by the trauma of surgery, complications, four weeks in a hospital bed, and whatever else happened inside. I now struggled to raise my own derriere. *Certainly, this physical therapist's medical knowledge lacked seriously in the area in which I suffered*, I thought. However, his instruction, encouragement and motivation helped me realize that this part of my recovery required my personal effort – effort based upon my faith in what God had done and was still doing. Several times a day, I determined to make the choice to believe, and try. Several times a day, it was up to me to try. And try I did!

As the days passed, I witnessed a miracle. My strength increased, and eventually, I lifted my own butt! Not only this, but as the days and weeks passed, I celebrated new milestones. The day I gained enough strength to stand at the bathroom sink and brush my own teeth, I danced the best I could with my limited, but improving ability. The day I stood at the bathroom sink and brushed my teeth and washed my face consecutively, I had a praise party all by myself. The day, with Shawn's help, I stepped into the shower, sat on the shower seat my dear friend Deidra sent, let's just say was simply refreshing.

Over a month previously passed since I enjoyed a shower; hearing this, my loving friend and prayer partner ordered and sent me a shower bench, "You will take a shower!" Understanding the importance of this hygienic right, she expressed shipped a blessing to my doorstep. Lovingly, Shawn assembled it, covered the drains, holes, and wounds on my abdomen and chest and scrubbed off the month-long buildup of dead skin layering my body. With the special oil my mother-in-law Dee sent, Shawn massaged the wife whose body looked so different than on our wedding night. He lived his vows to me in ways I never imagined he would ever need to.

Each milestone of recovery brought with it a new reason to be thankful and served as fuel to keep me encouraged and striving for further progress. Little did I know, like clay in a potter's hand, God held me, made me over, and gave me a deeper level of faith. Five months of recovery passed before I stood in the pulpit to share a much-abbreviated sermon, a departure from my usual 30 minute or more oration. Twelve months passed before I could physically manage a full- time workload. Twenty-four months passed before feeling more like myself again, managing home, life, and work. While my body, mind, and spirit endured a tremendous trauma, I needed this time off desperately. Though sudden and horrific, what happened to me made room for God's work through me and time for God's revelation to me. What I discovered while enduring this tragedy guided me out triumphantly. By the grace of God, I can now say, my struggle was worth it.

PART II

Discoveries

DISCOVERY 1

REMEMBER THAT?

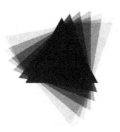

"I guess I'll never wear a bikini," I said to my parents as I gazed at my reflection in the mirror. I was about 12 years old, and I don't think my parents wanted their pre-teen daughter to wear a bikini anyway. The scar that ran up the length of my abdomen was ugly and embarrassing as a teen. The hardened skin covered the story of my survival as an infant. With time, I grew to love that scar and the story as my parents told me.

My young parents were brave immigrants from Jamaica who had migrated with the dream of building a better life for themselves and their children. They started with very little, as had many immigrants like them in the sixties and seventies. By their early thirties, they were already homeowners, caring for a family with four children. Just a few months after I was born, I became terribly sick and my parents were unexpectedly hurled into a trial and test of their faith.

After numerous medical exams, it was determined that something was wrong with my tender six-month-old heart. The night before my surgery, a critical sample was spilled and the procedure was cancelled. Further investigation led the doctors away from their initial hypothesis of a heart condition and it was determined I didn't need the surgery.

As the symptoms remained unresolved, the next step was exploratory surgery. If left untreated, the doctors said I could live up to12 years as the demand upon my heart was too great. However, if operated upon, I had a 50/50 chance of survival. Mom bravely took the pen, praying with all the faith she had, and signed the consent for the surgery.

I survived. Now, as a fully aware adult, I would find myself in a life-threatening situation again. While lying in that hospital bed, I looked at the first scar that told the story of God's past miracles. The scar had become so much a part of me, that I stopped rehearsing the story, and simply put it out of my mind. Lying in that hospital bed; however, I remembered. God rewarded my mother's faith and saved my life. I lived far beyond those twelve years. I had gone from the monkey bars on the playground to the asphalt on the track. I experienced landing on the sand in the triple jump and running long jump pit, even trying out the shot-put ball. As I grew up, I was not limited. If God saved my life before, He could do it again!

Looking at myself, still with two JP drains, one PICC line and abdominal wounds, I needed to experience God more fully as my healer. I wanted to be whole. I needed those tubes gone and wounds healed. So, with renewed faith, I read the Gospel accounts of Jesus healing others. Then it dawned on me as it never had before, Jesus healed people that came to him and asked in faith. Jesus healed everyday ordinary people! He healed men and women, young and old, rich, and poor. He even raised the dead when deemed best! Jesus healed people, regular people over 2000 years ago.

I believed Jesus is alive and in Heaven interceding for me, the same as He was then. So, I said, "Jesus, will you heal my abscesses and rid me of these drainage tubes?" I placed my hands on my abdomen, while looking at my dry skin shriveling around the JP tubes. I prayed further, "Lord, you healed others before, please heal me." Now, as I reviewed what Christ performed before, in faith I truly believed Hebrews 13:8, "Jesus Christ is the same yesterday and today and forever." If he did it before, He sure can do it again!

DISCOVERY 2

WAIT A MINUTE...I'M HEALED?

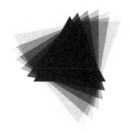

L ord, this is tough. I prayed, looking at my bedridden self as I lay attached to multiple lines and tubes in the hospital. *I'm in my late 30's, 40 does not seemed promised*, I contemplated. Months before all of this ensued, I knew I was heading into a life storm and was impressed that I would be okay, but this seemed way too dreadfully close to death's door. Then I got his voicemail. My colleague and friend, Pastor Lee left me the words from Isaiah 53 that would later bolster my faith during periods of doubting:

"But He was wounded for our transgressions, He was bruised for our iniquities; the chastisement for our peace was upon Him, and by His stripes we are healed" (Isaiah 53:5).

Very familiar with this passage, I recited it many times for others, now I recited it for me. It would later be the foundation of yet another truth on my journey to triumph—remember what God has said.

Throughout the many months of my illness and recuperation, at times, I experienced emotional lows. I remembered what God had accomplished before, but did that automatically mean He would do it again? I could not believe what was happening to me, so sudden and unwelcomed. How would I survive this? I could not work, neither think about the matters of the church, or even the matters of my house. Once at home, when not attempting my exercises or resting, I simply sat propped up in bed listening to worship songs, reading the Bible, and praying. I did these things not for the purpose of sermon preparation, or sharing, but simply for personal edification, transformation and revelation. Simply for me. Then one day, within a few weeks of recuperating at home, I pulled out my cell phone and listened to Pastor Lee's message again. I grabbed my Bible and rediscovered that familiar passage: "...by His stripes we are healed." *Wait a minute... I'm healed? I'm healed!*

There it was again, faith. Like a surge of electricity illuminating my mind, I believed. I recalled being impressed by the Holy Spirit in prayer months before this tragedy, that I would be okay. Now this very passage of Scripture arose as confirmation. Jesus took the punishment, so I could be made well, not just my congregation, or someone I visited in the hospital or nursing facility, but me. By His stripes, *I* am healed. Then it hit me, there was more to this than future salvation from sin. Jesus' death on the cross served not only to save me from sin making me whole spiritually, but physically as well. Then somehow, I stumbled upon another verse:

"that it might be fulfilled which was spoken by Isaiah the prophet, saying: 'He

Himself took our infirmities and bore our sicknesses'" (Matthew 8:17).

After Jesus healed Peter's mother-in-law of her fever, others brought many later that evening to be healed by Jesus. With a Word, Jesus freed the demon-possessed and healed all who were sick. Matthew 8:17, gives the explanation that the Scripture in Isaiah was being fulfilled! *He makes me, Tricia, whole not only spiritually, but physically as well.* I repeated this passage over and over again. The more I repeated it, the more I believed it.

God assured me that I would be okay in more than one way. I was prayerfully anointed three times, and twice over the very area that would later be injured. The Holy Spirit impressed me in prayer, months before my illness that I would be alright and my God-fearing community of faith believed for me, even when I could not believe for myself. Taking a bar of soap, I wrote on my bathroom mirror, "I am healed!" When tempted to feel low as the days, weeks, and months passed, I would think, *I am healed,* then say out loud, "I am healed!" I declared, "I will be okay!"

DISCOVERY 3

YOU NEED TO PRAISE MORE!

"We're Expression of Praise and we've come to let you know that Jesus is: worthy! Jesus is worthy! Jesus is worthy! Worthy to be praised!" We rocked and swayed in our robes, elbows popping up from side to side as our young teenage voices bellowed and sang at the top of our lungs. The choir became an extended family and the place where I grew in my own faith as a teenager, singing even when I didn't feel like it. I would never have imagined how critical my time in the teen and youth choir would be for my spiritual growth and formation. Every Friday night we gathered for rehearsal, whether we were scheduled to sing for the next day's service or not. During a particular rehearsal a spiritual mentor said, "Tricia, you need to praise God more! Be thankful!" I'm not sure how I must have been looking that day, but that lesson stuck with me and I remembered it as I fought for my life.

"Every praise is to our God, every word of worship on one accord, every praise, every praise is to our God..." Music rang out from my bedroom constantly once I made it home from the hospital. Gospel, or worship and praise music streamed non-stop. In these times however, it was not simply background music. I listened to the words, and the songs became my praise and my prayer. Unbeknownst to me, God was solidifying another vital strategy. To guard my mind, I needed to maintain an attitude of praise and gratitude. Proverbs 4:23 says, "Watch over your heart with all diligence, for from it flow the springs of life" (NASB). Especially in these moments of battle, I needed to maintain full confidence in God as He was and is the only one who could pull me out in victory. There is so much God desires to do for us, so much He desires to give, but at times our minds are preoccupied and filled with everything else but confidence and hope in God. Whatever would maintain and grow my faith in God was what I permitted my mind to dwell on.

Worshipping in this way, coupled with my incessant jubilation over new milestones achieved and prayers answered, barricaded my mind from depression and despair as I awaited full recovery. The abscesses began healing, and one of the JP tubes was removed. However, another drainage tube and fistula remained. My abdominal wounds were closing but were still not fully healed. I could not give up. Remaining thankful for the small blessings and keeping a song in my heart, helped me maintain my faith in what He had done in the past, and in what He said. There were, however, difficult moments, even with the praise music playing, that I

75

simply froze in front of the mirror attempting to perform my dressing changes and wound cleaning. I could not believe what I saw in the mirror. My abdomen appeared butchered. I was stuck.

Noticing my temporary paralysis, Shawn pried me away from the bathroom mirror and coached me through moving 12 feet from the bathroom mirror to the bedroom. There is no way I could have triumphed through this without him and the community of loving family, friends, and church family. I soon realized the next vital key to triumphing over tragedy–remain with people of faith and love.

DISCOVERY 4

NOT ALL BY MYSELF

The front door looked like a mile away from where we sat. When we first pulled into the parking lot upon my first discharge to home, December's Midwest winter wonderland of cold proved merciless to our frightful plight. *How in the world would I get from the car to the house?* Standing arm locked in arm with Shawn, slowly, we took one step and then another. Just less than two years prior to this moment, we locked arms as we walked from the altar to our new lives as Mr. & Mrs. Payne. We were happy newlyweds spending most days finding something to laugh about, dating at least weekly, and taking exciting adventures to Canada, and to the Caribbean. We enjoyed each other. Now, the future appeared uncertain. Shawn, unbeknownst to me left his contract traveling position with his company to stay home and care for me. With looming medical bills, and daily living expenses, this was a step of faith and love. Shawn having no medical experience to provide care for a sick wife, would soon learn by crash course, to be a nurse, doctor, and emotional support all wrapped up in one.

I felt so nervous during those initial days at home. I could only imagine how Shawn was feeling. Now, he would be solely responsible for my care. Our tender marriage of just one year met a great test. I can't imagine Shawn would have ever dreamed that just after a year and a half of saying, "I do," to better or worse, in sickness and health, his word would be tested. But God sustained him and me. I know now, this was only in response to prayer and the loving support of a good community.

Prayers were ascending for us around the clock and around the world. My near 95-year-old, faith-filled grandmother prayed, our parents prayed, our siblings, aunts, uncles, nieces, and extended family prayed. Our friends prayed. Our churches and church administration prayed. Mentors and supporters prayed. Not only was there a community of people praying, agreeing for my healing and our help, but people lent physical and emotional support. Friends sent flowers, cards, helpful gifts, and natural aromatherapy remedies. The church community sent food when I could tolerate it. Friends, pastors, and church family visited. I had a core of close friends that communicated with me regularly, encouraging me and praying for me. My Dad, Courtney, always warned as we grew up, "Be careful of the company you keep!"

Each Sunday after dinner, Dad took the time to have a family meeting with his growing children. His main purpose? To instill principles for success in our minds. One lesson he repeated weekly, "Keep good company!" He cautioned us about the danger of,

"Bad company." In his own way he echoed the teaching of Scripture, "He who walks with wise men will be wise, but the companion of fools will be destroyed" (Proverbs 13:20).

I learned when facing life-storms, I needed to be surrounded with, "good company." To triumph, I needed to keep people of faith near me. A wise man once said, "Two are better than one, because they have a good reward for their labor. For if they fall, one will lift up his companion. But woe to him who is alone when he falls, for he has no one to help him up" (Ecclesiastes 4:9-10).

I had a lower chance of surviving this adversity alone. Stories I read in the Bible also reveal this truth. Whether it was leading others effectively, or coping with death and loss, finding love or escaping murder plots, and death threats, even in averting a national genocide, people relied on the help of other trusted individuals. I needed my family, friends, and church community. Before heading into the hospital, I gave Shawn a list of names and numbers – a few of my closest friends, sisters and prayer warriors – my emergency contacts. "These are the people to notify if anything goes wrong," I said. I could count on them to pray me through. We practiced interceding for each other countless times before, and now was no different. I needed to stay with people of faith and love.

WHAT DID YOU SAY YOUR NAME WAS AGAIN?

My little manual shift Honda Civic packed to capacity, my friend and former pastor, John, drove as I reclined in the passenger seat. Meanwhile his best friend Daniel drove behind us, his CRV filled with the rest of my belongings. It was June 2005, just three years after graduation from physical therapy school and now all roads led to Andrews University Seventh-day Adventist

Theological Seminary in Michigan. God had called me to make this life-altering step to leave everything behind and pursue His will, and I was grateful for John and Daniel's help on my journey.

Together we drove 500 miles from Toronto to Southwest Michigan, full of hope and joy about what was ahead of us. I don't remember exactly when I noticed the metal "L" shaped bar detach from the 16-wheeler in front of us and come hurtling toward John and I in my Civic. All I know is that our happy chatter immediately stopped, and we watched in helpless horror. The bar bounced a few times almost in slow motion as it headed directly for the driver's side windshield. Certainly, by the combination of our speed, the speed of that iron bar and our collision trajectory, we were destined for a terrible accident and personal injury. I may have struggled to get an 'A' in physics but figuring this out was not difficult. We did not have time to swerve, change lanes, or avoid this inevitable impact. The bar was headed right for us, unyielding as we accelerated over 70 miles an hour. I didn't have time to get on my knees, find a Bible verse, breathe a long sentence or whisper a prayer. Instead, my faith gripped my spirit and I said one word, "Jesus!"

When the metal bar made contact, the glass windshield did not shatter. Instead the glass became as plastic, absorbed the impact and then bowed out pushing the metal bar out, up and away. We were awestruck. We just witnessed a miracle! Shaking and praying, we pulled over to assess the damage and to catch our breath. We hadn't imagined this. The windshield had not broken. Nothing on the car was damaged except for a small scratch on the hood and roof of the car.

God spared us as simply as I called on the name of Jesus! This was one of my first experiences with having awareness of the power of Jesus' name. Later, I came to understand the true importance of knowing and trusting God's name.

As 1 John 5:14-15 says, "Now this is the confidence that we have in him, that if we ask anything according to His will, He hears us. And if we know that He hears us, whatever we ask, we know that we have the petitions that we have asked of Him."

Before November 28, 2017, I merely believed the truth of this Scripture cognitively, but by April 2018, I knew the truth of this text experientially because I grew to understand more about God's name. How? My friend told me she was praying Psalm 91 for me.

My dear friend and long-time prayer partner, Deidra sent me a text message soon after my second discharge home, "We're praying Psalm 91 for you." Years prior, I committed this Psalm to memory at the prompting of a mentor and prayer warrior. Now, years later, Deidra said she and my loving friend Chanda were claiming this Psalm on my behalf. With peaked curiosity, I propped myself up in bed and turned to Psalm 91. This time something caught my attention and jumped off the page. My heart beat faster, I felt compelled to re-read verse 14,

"Because he has set his love upon Me, therefore I will deliver him; I will set him on high, because he has known My name."

Your name Lord? Silently questioning. What does it mean to know Your name? Immediately, I recalled a story in Exodus 34 where a frustrated Moses went up to the Mountain of the Lord, Mount Sinai, a second time. After destroying the first stone tablet of God's handwritten Ten Commandments at the sight of the people's obstinate display of disobedience, Moses had to again ascend Mount Sinai at God's instruction for God to rewrite His commandments on tablets of stone Moses this time, had to carve.

Before God re-wrote His commandments, He first introduced Himself, proclaiming His own name, "The Lord, the Lord God, merciful and gracious, longsuffering, and abounding in goodness and truth..." Exodus 34:6. I knew this story and knew the verses that came next, but I could not read past this verse. "The Lord, the Lord God, merciful and gracious..." I repeated it over and over, studied the Hebrew, and concluded, Lord, I have not truly known Your name!

Prior to this hospitalization and subsequent recovery time at home, I believed in

God. I knew He existed and believed whole-heartedly that God created the world. I believed that God sent Jesus Christ, His Son to save the world, and that Jesus is coming again. I believed in God, but I did not fully believe correctly about the nature of God's heart. Faith in God is not merely to believe that He exists, but to truly believe the right thing about His nature and character. As the New Living Translation puts it, "Yahweh! The Lord! The God of compassion and mercy! I am slow to anger and filled with un-failing love and faithfulness..." (Exodus 34:6).

God is compassionate. He cares about what I am going through. That's who He is! Words feel insufficient to describe the impact that this realization had upon my broken spirit. It felt like God wrapped my aching heart in the balm of His love as I accepted this revelation. His peace and joy blanketed me. At my moment of understanding, I rested my hand upon my yet to be healed wounds, and like a one-year-old stretching her hands up to her Daddy with the expectation that he will lift her up and carry her in his arms, I prayed with expectation. In full faith and assurance in the merciful love and gracious kindness of my God, I prayed. Heal me Lord. This time my prayer was different than any previous prayer I uttered for myself during my hospitalization. I prayed with heartfelt expectation and trust in the goodness, mercy and kindness of my God. I prayed with saving faith. I knew, even before seeing it, that I would receive good from the hand of God. Without fully realizing it many years before, I had said the name of Jesus with similar faith right before that metal bar bounced off my windshield. I had come full circle.

When we are in grave pain, it is in our nature to become distracted by our discomfort. We may even view the entire world through the lens of our adverse circumstances. When our pain is all we see, the bigger picture becomes distorted and so does our image of God. So instead of coming to Him in faith, we come in fear and doubt. Instead of coming up from our knees saying Amen in peace, we feel even worse as we wonder if He truly cares enough to help. Hebrews 11:6 says, "...for he who comes to God must believe that He is..." Not only did I believe that He exists, but discovered He is who He says He is.

DISCOVERY 6

DON'T STOP

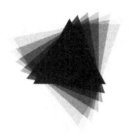

"Now let's kneel down, clasp our hands and pray. Repeat after me: *Now I lay me down to sleep, I pray the Lord my soul to keep and if I die before I wake, I pray the Lord my soul to take. Amen.*"

My parents taught us to pray at an early age. As Jamaicans, they were both raised in God-fearing homes. Dad and Mom brought us to church each Sunday as children. We went to either that big white brick mega church on the west end of the city or the brown brick Bible Chapel down the street from our home. I especially liked the Bible Chapel because Sunday school was simply fun. I learned there that Jesus is Lord and memorized my first Bible verse, "For God so loved the world that He gave His only begotten Son, that whosoever believes in Him should not perish but have everlasting life" (John 3:16).

On one particular Sunday, they gave all the children a rainbow sticker that had the words on it, "Jesus is Lord." I stuck it to my dresser drawer in my bedroom, and every day I just stared at it and repeated over and over, "Jesus is Lord... Jesus is Lord... Jesus is Lord..." Until one day, it clicked! My young mind awaked from a masked stupor to the reality of a Divine Being that assumed total responsibility for me. Feeling deep joy, I sat in awe. For the first time, I experienced personal faith in Christ. I started to pray not just before bed, upon waking or at mealtime, but about what I observed at school and how it made me feel.

"Dear Jesus," I prayed, kneeling by my bedside with hands clasped, *"You see, on the playground my friends' hair blows in the*

wind and my hair doesn't. Please let my hair grow so that it will blow in the wind too. " As I write this now, I'm doubled over in laughter. God must have smiled too.

To my grateful amazement, my hair did grow, and as my mom clipped the ends of my plaits and ponytails with barrettes, my hair eventually flowed in the wind. I'm still laughing while writing this. For the record, I have grown to love my hair in all its forms: braided relaxed, natural, ponytail or even under a sew-in. Nevertheless, as a child, I started praying about the things that bothered me. Later, due to my grandmother's influence, we started attending a Sabbath-keeping church on Saturday's. Here at the Seventh-day Adventist church, my faith, knowledge of Scripture and prayer life continued to grow. I am so glad that my parents taught us at an early age to pray and look to God for ultimate help in all things. Now in what evolved into a terrible tragedy, I needed not just to pray once, but persistently and at every turn this unexpected crisis took, especially as it pertained to that stubborn fistula.

Matthew 7: 7-11 in the NLT says, "Keep on asking, and you will receive what you ask for. Keep on seeking and you will find. Keep on knocking, and the door will be opened to you. For everyone who asks, receives. Everyone who seeks finds. And to everyone who knocks, the door will be opened. You parents – if your children ask for a loaf of bread, do you give them a stone instead? Or if they ask for a fish do you give them a snake? Of course not! So if you sinful people know how to give good gifts to your children, how much more will your heavenly Father give good gifts to those who ask him?"

Now, I determined to keep on asking, seeking, and knocking down Heaven's door for complete healing. Jesus gives assurance in His word that if we continue to petition Him in faith that He will answer. So, I kept on asking. Believing in God's name, I kept asking. Remembering what God performed in the past, I kept asking. Remembering what God promised me, I kept asking. Guarding my thoughts, remaining in an atmosphere of praise and thanksgiving, I kept asking. Staying in the company of people of faith and love, we kept asking. We all continued to persist in prayer not because I believe God needs to be massaged and melted, but because I learned a while ago that prayer doesn't change God, it changes us.

However long, God wanted to take to bring me and Shawn through this life storm, was necessary time to work in us something far greater than I could imagine or think. Scripture says this, "My brethren, count it all joy when you fall into various trials, knowing that the testing of your faith produces patience. But let patience have its perfect work, that you may be perfect and complete, lacking nothing" (James 1: 2-4). God was making me better. God was making us better. Our marriage grew stronger, our love for each other deepened, our characters were being refined under God's molding hand.

The lessons through this tragedy transformed me. While I learned about prayer as a child and continued to grow in my understanding of prayer as a teen and young adult, I have never been so aware of the manifest impact of prayer as when negotiating this life storm. Just ask! Keep on asking. No matter how bad it got, I kept asking.

DISCOVERY 7

SCIENCE ISN'T FINAL

BEEP! BEEP! BEEP! BEEP!

My chest pounded and my heart raced, threatening to jump right out of my chest. Pain gripped my body mercilessly, holding on. Pain imprisoned me, I felt powerless to stop what was happening. The room suddenly swarmed with white coats and green scrubs moving in intense fury. What was all of the fuss about? It was about me!

The tension in the room thickened by the second, I couldn't believe this was happening. *Was this all an overreaction?* I wondered. The expression on their faces, all directed at me, answered my question. This was a fatal emergency. Fright overwhelmed me as I looked at Shawn. Appearing just as concerned, Shawn gazed at me seemingly helpless to change what unfolded. Something was terribly wrong. The doctor swept my room with haste and explained, "We have to reset her heart. Where's the husband?" Shawn raised his hand, "Right here!"

"Okay," the doctor said, "it's your job to keep her here."

Shawn, gazed into my eyes, held my hand, and started talking as the room buzzed with what seemed like the entire staff from the floor. Directing his attention toward me, the physician explained, "Now Tricia, this will probably hurt. It won't feel good."

Shawn continued his conversation with me, distracting me from this imminent heart pausing procedure. "One, two, three..." Suddenly I felt nothing. I heard nothing. I sensed nothing. I said nothing. A brief moment of absolutely nothing as my heart slowed to a near halt. "Tricia?" Then, I heard my name.

Just as suddenly as everything stopped, it started all over again. "That did not hurt at all!" I said nearly oblivious to what just happened. My heart raced furiously out of rhythm beating near 200 beats per minute requiring chemical cardioversion.

Finally, it was concluded that I indeed became septic as a result of a bowel perforation during what was supposed to be a simple outpatient procedure. I required emergency small bowel repair; my future appeared uncertain. This was life threatening. People have died from such injuries. My prognosis was unclear and my progress to a full recovery not promised by medical personnel.

"When will this one heal?" I said pointing at the fistula that formed through my abdominal incision. "Oh, that one? Well we don't know. That one could take a while...some never heal." The physician's response saddened me.

Perhaps one of the most visually horrifying complications of this emergency surgery was the formation of the abdominal fistula. Putrid bowel contents poured out from my abdomen requiring a catheter bag. The two

JP tubes drained remnants of infected fluid from the abscess that had formed along my left abdominal cavity. They were horrifying enough, but not more so than that fistula. Countless times, Shawn found me standing in front of the bathroom mirror frozen as I attempted to change my dressings, paralyzed by the sight of the fistula.

Now it needs to be said, having a fistula is not a reason to remain hospitalized or bed-ridden at home. It is unsightly but has minimal impact on day to day activities. Life can go on with a fistula, but that wasn't the type of life I wanted to lead.

Believing the right thing about God's character, I laid my hands over each JP tube and watched miraculously as the abscesses healed, but the fistula stubbornly remained. Remembering what God did in the past, I prayed and watched my abdominal incision heal, but that fistula would not. Remembering what God said, I prayed and the PICC line was discontinued, but the fistula just would not close. Guarding my mind, remaining grateful, I praised and enjoyed eating food again, but that fistula just would not heal. Staying with people of faith and of love, we prayed, and I gained increasing strength weekly, but that fistula just would not close. I persisted in prayer and was able to bathe myself with little assistance, but that fistula would not heal. I had yet to uncover by experience one final truth in triumphing through tragedy – Jesus has the final say, even over my body.

It is a commonly held belief that the words of authority figures carry lasting impact. For instance, what a parent says to their child, or a teacher to a student, physicians to patients, and even clergy to a parishioner may stay with them for life. A doctor's spoken prognosis if believed, has the power to help people heal when positive, or when negative may lead to depression. My doctor said that this fistula may never heal. In other words, the contents of my bowels might always ooze through my abdomen. I would have to live with this hole, changing poopy dressing as a way of life. Just how would this work as a newlywed? Would science have the last word?

But in ever increasing faith, I remembered what God said. *Jesus was wounded for my transgressions, bruised for my iniquities, that the chastisement of my peace was upon Him, by His stripes I am healed!* Remembering what God said, I laid my hand over my abdomen, over the wound that would not heal, and prayed and prayed and prayed, *Jesus, please heal me.*

Remembering what God had been doing - my heart began beating in correct rhythm and I returned to my pre-admission weight. The doctors discontinued the tube feed and real food once again crossed my lips. I could take a bath, brush my teeth, and make a hair appointment. Each step showed God's healing. God saved my life 40 years ago and I believed He was not through with me yet; He had yet more life to give.

Oh yes, I want to praise Him for who He is and what He has done for me! As I prayed with my sisters, I was reminded that God is compassionate and cares ever so much about me. I laid my hands over my cured abdomen and I believe God wanted to heal me.

I wish I could say that the fistula closed instantaneously the day I believed God's name but it did not. However, each day the edges moved closer and closer together. God provided an answer. He taught me to be patient! I saw it happening before my eyes. With much prayer and ointment received from a discerning physical therapist, the last opening finally closed! What I did not know, was that this particular wound coupled with my painful journey, would reinforce an important reality in being able to triumph through tragedy. Regardless of what anyone says, even above science, Jesus has the final say. I managed to move from the surgical bed, to the cardiac ICU, to acute care, to home, to home with home nursing and physical therapy, to outpatient services and appointments and eventually back to work because Jesus has the final say in all things even in what may seem impossible.

The Psalmist David said, "I will worship toward Your holy temple, and praise Your name for Your lovingkindness and Your truth; for You have magnified Your word above all Your name" (Psalm 138:2). The

New Living Translation of the Bible, renders the last portion of this Scripture in this way, "...for your promises are backed by all the honor of your name." God's name, or reputation of his character is on the line should His word fail. In other words, His word will not fail. His character will not allow it. That's just who He is. The Psalm ends this way, "The Lord will work out his plans for my life – for your faithful love, O Lord, endures forever. Don't abandon me, for you made me" (Psalm 138:8). The Psalmist under the inspiration of the Holy Spirit, penned with complete confidence in the nature of God. No matter what, His Word stands. God's intention for us stands. God ultimately has the last Word. Jesus has the final say.

CONCLUSION

Whatever you might be going through today, my prayer is that you will see that God is near to help you through and make you better in the end. For me, I needed this time of transformation desperately. What happened to me, though sudden and horrific, made room for God's work in me. The struggle was worth it. What God performed in me, worked out of me, and revealed to me, made up for the pain of this tragedy. I needed this time alone with God desperately, for up until this point, ministry filled my days to the point of exhaustion. I did not practice good self-care and gave everything mentally, emotionally, and physically to my church responsibilities. Simply put, I was tired and running on empty, not knowing how to stop. Ministry, unlike any other profession, taxed me in a way I never knew possible. Just when I thought I could not continue, this tragedy offered me a reset. The days I spent studying the Bible and in prayer, rekindled a fire in me I did not know had fizzled.

With renewed motivation and drive, I eventually returned to work. Five months had passed since I last stood in my pulpit to preach, but this time was different. The time spent in worship during my period of recovery at home, calmed previous anxieties and I started ministering and living from a different spiritual space. At times, I am tempted to forget what happened, allowing the busyness of life to wash away the memory of those necessary truths learned.

My husband Shawn, family, and close friends have to help me recall what I went through, but writing this book for you, reinforces those life lessons. The words of James are so very true, "My brethren, count it all joy when you fall into various trials, knowing that the testing of your faith produces patience, but let patience have its perfect work, that you may be perfect and complete, lacking nothing" (James 1:2-4).

REFERENCES

Benedetti, Fabrizio. "How the doctor's words affect the patient's brain." Evaluation & the health
professions vol.25,4 (2002): 369-86. doi: 10.1177/0163278702238051

Blackaby, Henry, et al. *Experiencing God*. Macmillan Publishers, 2008.

New American Standard Bible. La Habra, CA: The Lockman Foundation, 1995. Digital.

New King James Version Holy Bible. Belgium: Thomas Nelson, 1990. Print.

New Living Translation Holy Bible. Wheaton, Ill: Tyndale House Publishers, 2004. Print.

Staton, LJ, et al. "When Race Matters: Disagreement in Pain Perception between Patients and Their Physicians in Primary Care." *Journal of the National Medical Association*, vol. 99, no. 5, 2007, pp. 532–38. *NCBI*, www.ncbi.nlm.nih.gov/pubmed/17534011.

"The Disturbing Reason Some African American Patients May Be Undertreated for Pain." *Washington Post* [U.S. & World], 4 Apr. 2016, www.washingtonpost.com/news/to-your-health/wp/2016/04/04/do-blacks-feel-less-pain-than-whites-their-doctors-may-think-so.

ABOUT THE AUTHOR

Tricia Wynn Payne is a highly sought after international Christian speaker and preacher, who has enjoyed sharing life-transforming messages of encouragement, empowerment, and hope for over 20 years. Inspired by suffering life-threatening complications after undergoing a minor outpatient procedure, she now seeks to advance the restoration of individuals facing adversity in all phases of life.

She transitioned from a nine-year career as physical therapist to serve full-time in pastoral ministry. As a physical therapist she served internationally, assisting in the rehabilitation of individuals in intensive care, acute care, and outpatient clinical settings. She also guest-lectured, mentored, and assisted in the instruction of physical therapy students.

Because of her passion to inspire others with the life empowering message of God's love as expressed in the Bible, Tricia embraced the invitation to work as a full-time pastor. In this capacity, she has initiated innovative youth and young adult focused ministries, developed community partnerships, and created outreach programs to assist underprivileged, at-risk, and refugee populations.

While conducting young adult outreach in Chicago Illinois, she met Kansas City, Missouri native Shawn Payne, who would later become the love of her life and husband. Together they reside in Metro Detroit Michigan.

CPSIA information can be obtained
at www.ICGtesting.com
Printed in the USA
BVHW051531050821
613735BV00011B/1060